Puff-Puff, Chugga-Chugga

CHRISTOPHER WORMELL

MARGARET K. McELDERRY BOOKS

NEW YORK   LONDON   TORONTO   SYDNEY   SINGAPORE

Once there was a little train that ran along a line
between the conductor's cottage and the town, and
back again. Some days were busy and some days
were not; you never could tell.

But one day the conductor thought, *I have a funny feeling today will be a busy one.*

And it was.

Puff-puff, chugga-chugga, puff-puff, chugga-chugga.

At Seaside Station Mrs. Walrus was waiting with her shopping bag. "Lovely day for a trip into town," she said as she climbed into the pink car.

Oh dear, thought the conductor, *she's very large.*
She won't fit.

But she did.

Puff-puff, chugga-chugga, puff-puff, chugga-chugga.

Down the line at Forest Station Mr. Bear was waiting with *his* shopping bag. "Morning, conductor. Morning, Mrs.Walrus," he said as he climbed into the yellow car.

Gracious me! thought the conductor. *What an enormous bear. He surely won't fit.*

But he did.

Puff-puff, chugga-chugga, puff-puff, chugga-chugga.

At the third station, which was Jungle,
Mrs. Elephant was waiting with her shopping bag.
Mrs. Elephant climbed into the blue car.

Help! thought the conductor. *She'll never squeeze in.*

But she did.

Pufff-pufff, ch-chugga-chugga, pufff-pufff, ch-chugga-chugga.

My poor little train, thought the conductor. *It will never pull such a heavy load.*

But it did.

And presently they arrived at Town Station, where the three animals got out and set off for the shops.

"Don't buy too much," called the conductor, a little worried. "We don't want to overload the train."

But, of course, they did.

Mrs. Walrus went to the fishmonger's and bought six hundred sardines. Mr. Bear went to the baker's and bought five white loaves, five brown loaves, and five long French loaves. Then he went to the grocer's next door and bought six large pots of honey.

Mrs. Elephant went to the greengrocer's and
bought apples, oranges, bananas, pears, plums,
peaches, strawberries, raspberries, gooseberries,
mulberries, melons, mangoes, quinces, dates,
and a large pumpkin.

Back at the station the conductor was dismayed. "Oh no!" he cried. "There's far too much, all that fruit and bread and honey, not to mention the fish. It will never fit!"

But it did.

Puff-puff, chugga-chugga, puff-puff, chugga-chugga.

"Not so much after all," said Mrs. Walrus as the little train set off.

"Easily done," said Mr. Bear.

"It's just a question of balance," added Mrs. Elephant.

All would have been well, but at that moment a bee crawled up Mrs. Elephant's trunk. If only she had not sneezed.

But she did.

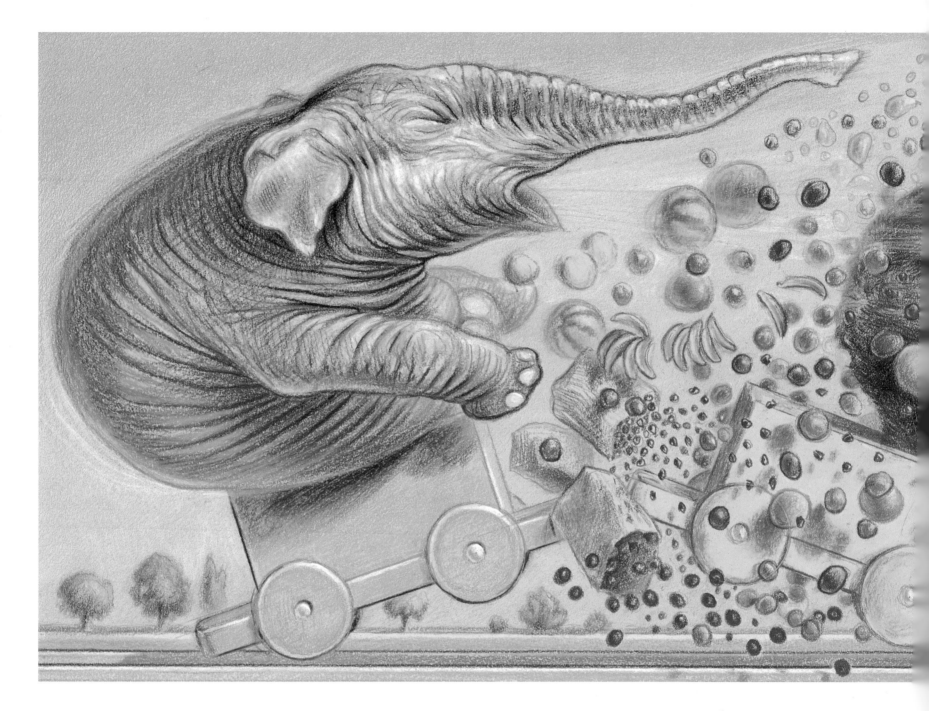

What a sneeze!

What a disaster!

"I told you so!" shouted the angry conductor.
"What are we going to do now?"

The animals looked around at all the food.

"Why not have a picnic?" said Mrs. Elephant.

"Excellent idea," said Mr. Bear.

"We can't eat all this. We need someone to share it with," said Mrs. Walrus.

"We'll have to call the others," said Mrs. Elephant.

So they did.

Mrs. Elephant lifted her trunk and trumpeted.
Mr. Bear whistled. Mrs. Walrus clapped her
flippers and bellowed.

What a racket!

After a while they stopped and listened. Faint and
far off they heard a rumble, which might have been
the sound of heavy animals on the move.

And it was.

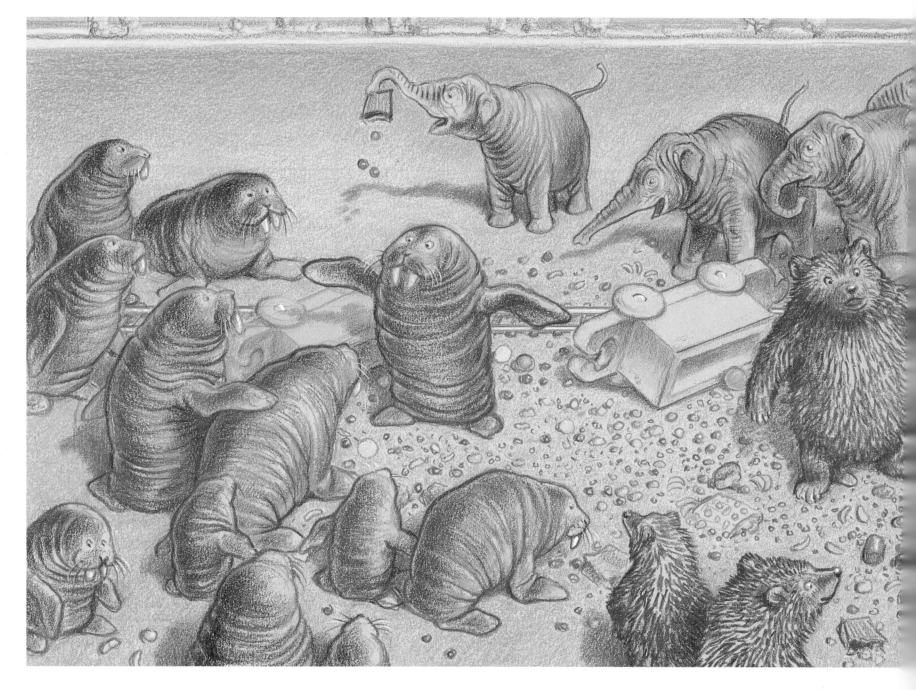

Presently a whole crowd of walruses and bears and elephants arrived at the side of the track.

"Anyone for a picnic?" invited Mrs. Elephant.

"Sardines all around," said Mrs. Walrus.

"Tuck in, everybody," said Mr. Bear.

And they did.

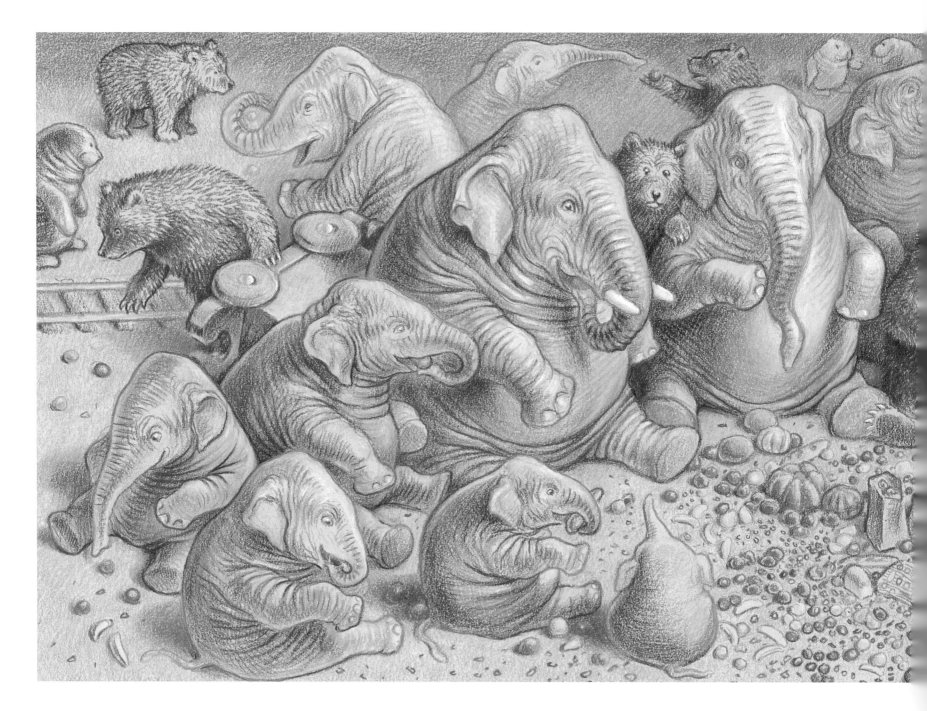

There had never been such a picnic.

There was plenty for everyone. The little elephants discovered banana sandwiches and the baby walruses tried bread and honey to see if they liked it. They did.

The little bears tried sardines, and they didn't.

Only the conductor was unhappy. "What about my train?" he cried.

"No problem," said Mrs. Walrus, lifting up the pink car with Mr. Walrus and the little ones lending a hand.

"Easily sorted out," said Mr. Bear. He and Mrs. Bear and the cubs heaved up the yellow car.

"It's just a question of leverage," said Mrs. Elephant, picking up the blue car with other elephants lending a trunk. "We'll have the train set to rights in no time at all."

And they did.

The conductor was still not happy. He had a nasty
feeling that all the animals might want a ride home.

But they didn't.

They were all far too full, and they dropped off to
sleep right where they were standing.

So as the sun sank over the sea the little train wound
its way homeward quite empty. *Puff-puff, chugga-chugga,
puff-puff, chugga-chugga.*

What a busy day. I shall sleep well tonight, thought the conductor.

And he did.

For Grandma May and Grandpa Jack

Margaret K. McElderry Books
An imprint of Simon & Schuster Children's Publishing Division
1230 Avenue of the Americas
New York, New York 10020

First published as *The Animal Train* in Great Britain by Jonathan Cape,
The Random House Group Limited
First United States Edition, 2001

Printed in Hong Kong

2 4 6 8 10 9 7 5 3 1

Library of Congress Card Catalog Number: 00-100370

ISBN 0-689-83986-3